C#

Advanced Features and Programming Techniques

Nathan Clark

Other Books in this Series

Computer Programming for Beginners

Fundamentals of Programming Terms and Concepts

a FREE Kindle Version with Paperback

C#

Programming Basics for Absolute Beginners

a FREE Kindle Version with Paperback

C#

A Detailed Approach to Practical Coding

a FREE Kindle Version with Paperback

Table of Contents

Introduction

Welcome to the third installment of the Step-By-Step C# series, where I go even further into the workings of C# by looking at advanced features and techniques. If you haven't read the first two books in the series, I highly suggest you do so before getting into this book.

C#

Programming Basics for Absolute Beginners

a, FREE Kindle Version with Paperback

C#

A Detailed Approach to Practical Coding

a, FREE Kindle Version with Paperback

An important aspect of this series, and your learning experience, is **learning by doing**. Practical examples are proven to be the best way to learn a programming language, which is why I have crammed as many examples into this guide as possible. I have tried to keep the core of the examples similar, so the only variable is the topic under discussion. This makes it easier to understand what we are implementing. As you progress through the chapters, remember to follow along with the examples and try them yourself.

With each topic in this advanced level guide, we will look at a detailed description, proper syntax and numerous examples to make your learning experience as easy as possible. C# is a powerful and versatile programming language and I trust you will enjoy this book as much as I enjoyed writing it.

So without further ado, let's get started!

1. Interfaces in C#

An interface is defined as a contract that is implemented by the class and available for use by other classes. An interface contains only the declaration of the functions. The method itself is defined by the class that inherits the method.

The definition of an interface is shown below.

```
public interface interfacename
{
// interface methods declaration
}
```

Then the necessary class would implement the interface accordingly.

```
class classname : interfacename
{
// interface method definition
}
```

Example 1: The following program is used to showcase how to use interfaces.

```
using System;
namespace Demo
```

```csharp
{
    // Defining the interface
    public interface Marks
    {
    // Declaring the interface methods
    void DisplayMarks();
    int Calculate();
    }
    public class Student : Marks
    {
        public int StudentID;
        public string StudentName;
        public int marks1,marks2;

        // Defining the interface methods
        public void DisplayMarks()
        {
            Console.WriteLine("The marks of subject 1 is " + marks1);
            Console.WriteLine("The marks of subject 2 is " + marks2);
        }
        public int Calculate()
        {
            return (marks1 + marks2);
        }
    }
    class Program
    {

        // The main function
        static void Main(string[] args)
        {
            Student stud1 = new Student();

            stud1.StudentID = 1;
            stud1.StudentName = "John";
            stud1.marks1 = 10;
            stud1.marks2 = 20;
```

```
        stud1.DisplayMarks();
        Console.WriteLine("The Total marks is " + stud1.Calculate());

      Console.Read();
        }
    }
}
```

With the above program:

- We can see that we are defining an interface class called 'Marks', which has a 'Display' method and a 'Calculate' method.

- We are then defining the implementation for these functions in the 'Student' class.

With this program, the output is as follows:

The marks of subject 1 is 10

The marks of subject 1 is 20

The Total marks is 30

We can also have a class inherit multiple interfaces at once. Let's look at an example of this.

Example 2: The following program is used to show how classes can use multiple interfaces.

```
using System;
namespace Demo
{
    // Defining the interface
    public interface Marks
      {
```

```csharp
   // Declaring the interface methods
   void DisplayMarks();
   int Calculate();
}

public interface location
{
   // Declaring the interface methods
   void InputCity(string city);
   void DisplayCity();
}

public class Student : Marks,location
{
   public int StudentID;
   public string StudentName;
   public int marks1,marks2;
   private string city;

   // Defining the interface methods
   public void InputCity(string pcity)
   {
      city = pcity;
   }

   public void DisplayCity()
   {
      Console.WriteLine("City is " + city);
   }

   public void DisplayMarks()
   {
      Console.WriteLine("The marks of subject 1 is " + marks1);
      Console.WriteLine("The marks of subject 2 is " + marks2);
   }

   public int Calculate()
```

```
        {
            return (marks1 + marks2);
        }
    }

class Program
{
    // The main function
    static void Main(string[] args)
    {

        Student stud1 = new Student();

        stud1.StudentID = 1;
        stud1.StudentName = "John";

        stud1.marks1 = 10;
        stud1.marks2 = 20;

        stud1.DisplayMarks();
        Console.WriteLine("The Total marks is " + stud1.Calculate());

        stud1.InputCity("New York");
        stud1.DisplayCity();

    Console.Read();
    }
  }
}
```

With the above program:

- We have defined 2 interfaces. The one is 'Marks' and the other is 'Location'.

- The 'Student' class takes on both the interfaces and also defines the methods of the interfaces accordingly.

With this program, the output is as follows:

The marks of subject 1 is 10

The marks of subject 1 is 20

The Total marks is 30

City is New York

1.1 Properties in Interfaces

Properties can also be defined in interfaces. The properties would then have either the 'get' or 'set' keyword, which would indicate whether the properties were read-only or read-write.

The syntax of the property definition in an interface is shown below.

```
public interface interfacename
    {
      // Property declaration:
      datatype propertyname
      {
        get;
        set;
      }
    }
```

If both the get and set methods are defined, it means that the property is a read-write property. Let's now look at an example of how properties in interfaces work.

Example 3: The following program shows how to use properties in interfaces.

```
using System;
namespace Demo
{
    // Defining the interface
    public interface Marks
        {
            // Read write property
        int marks
        {
            get;
            set;
        }
        // Read write property
        string Subject
        {
            get;
            set;
        }
        // Read only property
        int SubjectID
        {
            get;
        }
    }

    public class Student : Marks
    {
        public int StudentID;
        public string StudentName;

        public int marks  // read-write instance property
        {
            get
            {
```

```csharp
            return marks;
        }
        set
        {
            marks = value;
        }
    }

    public string Subject  // read-write instance property
    {
        get
        {
            return Subject;
        }
        set
        {
            Subject = value;
        }
    }

    public int SubjectID  // read-write instance property
    {
        get
        {
            return 1;
        }
    }
}

class Program
{
    // The main function
    static void Main(string[] args)
    {
        Student stud1 = new Student();

        stud1.StudentID = 1;
```

```
        stud1.StudentName = "John";

        stud1.marks = 10;
        stud1.Subject = "Subject1";

        Console.WriteLine("The marks is " + stud1.marks);
        Console.WriteLine("The Subject is " + stud1.Subject);
        Console.WriteLine("The SubjectID is " + stud1.SubjectID);

      Console.Read();
      }
    }
}
```

With the above program:

- We have set 3 properties in the interface.

- The 'Subject' and 'Marks' properties are read-write properties, because they have the 'get' and 'set' methods.

- The 'SubjectID' only has the 'get' property, so it is a read-only property.

- We then define the implementation of these properties in the class.

With this program, the output is as follows:

The marks is 10

The Subject is Subject1

The SubjectID is 1

2. Namespaces

Namespaces are used to logically separate functions that have the same name. So we could have two functions with the same name and same parameters, but with different functionality. Without the need to define classes, we can just segregate them into namespaces.

The syntax of a namespace is shown below.

```
namespace namespaceName
{
Class definition
{
// Define the functions
}
}
```

No matter which functions are defined, they will be part of the 'namespaceName' namespace. In some programs you would have the following definition.

```
using System;
```

Which results in using the functions that are defined in the 'System' namespace.

Example 4: The program below is used to showcase how to use namespaces.

```
using System;

// One namespace
namespace NameA{
   public class ClassA
   {
   public void FunctionA(){
      Console.WriteLine("This is namespace A");
   }
   }
}

// Second namespace
namespace NameB{
   public class ClassB
   {
      public void FunctionA()
      {
         Console.WriteLine("This is namespace B");
      }
   }
}

namespace Demo
{
      class Program
   {

      // The main function
      static void Main(string[] args)
      {
         // Using the namespaces
         NameA.ClassA clsA = new NameA.ClassA();
         clsA.FunctionA();
```

```
        NameB.ClassB clsB = new NameB.ClassB();
        clsB.FunctionA();

      Console.Read();
      }
    }
}
```

With the above program:

- We are defining 2 namespaces. The one is 'NameA' and the other is 'NameB'. Each namespace has a class defined and the same function defined.

- We can call each function via namespace in the main calling program.

With this program, the output is as follows:

This is namespace A

This is namespace B

We can also utilize the 'using' directive to use functions without the need to specify the namespace when calling the function. Let's look at an example of the using clause.

Example 5: This program is used to showcase how to use the using clause for namespaces.

```
using System;
using NameA;
using NameB;

// One namespace
namespace NameA{
   public class ClassA
```

```csharp
    {
    public void FunctionA(){
      Console.WriteLine("This is namespace A");
    }
    }
}

// Second namespace
namespace NameB{
    public class ClassB
    {
      public void FunctionA()
      {
        Console.WriteLine("This is namespace B");
      }
    }
}

namespace Demo
{
    class Program
    {

    // The main function
    static void Main(string[] args)
    {
      // Using the namespaces
      ClassA clsA = new ClassA();
      clsA.FunctionA();

      ClassB clsB = new ClassB();
      clsB.FunctionA();

    Console.Read();
    }
    }
}
```

With this program, the output is as follows:

This is namespace A

2.1 Nested Namespaces

Namespaces can also be nested, which means placing one namespace inside of another. The syntax of a simple nesting of namespaces is shown below.

```
namespace namespaceName1
{
Class definition
{
// Define the functions
}
namespace namespaceName2
{
Class definition
{
// Define the functions
}
}
}
```

Here we have 2 namespaces, one inside of another. Each function will be specific to the namespace it is defined in. So we can access Function A via the below code statement.

```
namespaceName1.FunctionA
```

And we can access Function B via the following code statement.

```
namespaceName1.namespaceName2.FunctionB
```

Example 6: The following program is used to show the way to use nested namespaces.

```
using System;

// One namespace
namespace NameA{
  public class ClassA
  {
  public void FunctionA(){
    Console.WriteLine("This is namespace A");
  }
  }
  // inner namespace
  namespace NameB
  {
    public class ClassB
    {
      public void FunctionA()
      {
        Console.WriteLine("This is namespace B");
      }
    }
  }
}

namespace Demo
{
    class Program
  {

    // The main function
    static void Main(string[] args)
    {
      // Using the namespaces
      NameA.ClassA clsA = new NameA.ClassA();
      clsA.FunctionA();
```

```
      NameA.NameB.ClassB clsB = new NameA.NameB.ClassB();
      clsB.FunctionA();

   Console.Read();
      }
   }
}
```

With the above program:

- We are defining 2 namespaces; 'NameA' and 'NameB'. Each namespace has the same function defined, but this time 'NameB' is defined inside of 'NameA'.

With this program, the output is as follows:

This is namespace A

This is namespace B

3. File I/O Operations

C# has a variety of classes that can be used in File I/O operations. It is important for any programming language to have support for File I/O operations and C# has that support built in.

The table below shows the various classes available in C# for I/O operations.

Table 1: File I/O Operations

Classes	Description
DriveInfo	Provides access to information on a drive
DirectoryInfo	Can provide more information of a particular directory
FileInfo	Can provide more information of a particular file
FileStream	Can be used to read the contents or write the contents to a file in bytes
StreamReader	Can be used to read data from a stream such as a file
StreamWriter	Can be used to write data from a stream such as a file

Classes	Description
StringReader	Enables you to read a string synchronously or asynchronously
StringWriter	Enables you to write a string synchronously or asynchronously

Let's now look at each function in greater detail.

3.1 DriveInfo

This class can provide more information pertaining to each drive on the local system.

Example 7: The following program shows how to use the DriveInfo class.

```
using System;
using System.IO;

namespace Demo
{
    class Program
    {

    // The main function
    static void Main(string[] args)
    {
        DriveInfo[] allDrives = DriveInfo.GetDrives();

        foreach (DriveInfo d in allDrives)
        {
            Console.WriteLine("Drive {0}", d.Name);
```

```
        Console.WriteLine(" Drive type: {0}", d.DriveType);
      }
    Console.Read();
      }
  }
}
```

With this program, the output is as shown below. The output will however vary from system to system.

Drive C:

Drive type:Fixed

Drive D:

Drive type:Fixed

3.2 DirectoryInfo

This class can provide more information pertaining to a particular directory.

Example 8: The following program is used to showcase the usage of the DirectoryInfo class.

```
using System;
using System.IO;

namespace Demo
{
    class Program
  {

      // The main function
```

```
        static void Main(string[] args)
        {

            DirectoryInfo di = new DirectoryInfo(@"E:\Project");
            Console.WriteLine("Does the directory exist " + di.Exists);
            Console.WriteLine("The creation time of the directory is "
+di.CreationTime);

            Console.Read();
        }
    }
}
```

With this program, the output is as shown below. Again, the output will vary from system to system.

Does the directory exist True

The creation time of the directory is 04/28/2017 11:12

3.3 FileInfo

This class can provide more information pertaining to a particular file.

Example 9: The program below showcases the way to use the FileInfo class.

```
using System;
using System.IO;

namespace Demo
{
    class Program
    {
```

```
      // The main function
      static void Main(string[] args)
      {

          FileInfo fi = new FileInfo(@"G:\Hello.html");
          Console.WriteLine("Does the file exist " + fi.Exists);
          Console.WriteLine("The creation time of the file is "
+fi.CreationTime);

          Console.WriteLine("The size of the file is " + fi.Length);

      Console.Read();
        }
     }
}
```

With this program the output is as shown below, and will vary from system to system.

Does the directory exist True

The creation time of the directory is 04/28/2017 11:12

The size of the file is 73

3.4 FileStream

This class can be used to read the contents of a file or write contents to a file. Note that this class works with the file in bytes. The general syntax when creating a new object of this class is given below.

```
FileStream fileobj = new FileStream("nameoffile",Options)
```

Where the options can be any one, or a combination of, the following:

- Append - It opens an existing file and puts the cursor at the end of file. It will alternatively create the file, if the file does not exist.

- Create - It creates a new file.

- CreateNew - It specifies to the operating system, that it should create a new file.

- Open - It opens an existing file.

- OpenOrCreate - It tells the operating system to open a file if it exists, otherwise it creates a new file.

- Truncate - It opens an existing file and truncates its size to zero bytes.

The steps for reading contents from a file using the FileReader class is shown below:

- First use the FileStream class to open the file with one of the abovementioned options.

- When you read from the file, you will get an array of bytes. Hence this should be stored in a byte array.

- The byte array then needs to be converted to a string and then displayed in the console.

Let's look at an example of how to use the Filereader class.

Example 10: The next program is used to showcase the way to use the FileStream class.

```csharp
using System;
using System.IO;
namespace Demo
{
    class Program
  {

    // The main function
    static void Main(string[] args)
    {

        // Opening the file in read only mode
        FileStream src = new
FileStream(@"G:\Hello.html",FileMode.Open, FileAccess.Read);

        // Number of bytes in the file
        int numBytes = (int)src.Length;
        // This will be used to get the number of bytes read
        int i = 0;
        // Storing the bytes in an array
        byte[] bytes = new byte[src.Length];

        Console.WriteLine("Number of bytes in the file " +
numBytes);

        src.Read(bytes, i, numBytes);

        string result = System.Text.Encoding.UTF8.GetString(bytes);
        Console.WriteLine(result);
      Console.Read();
      }
  }
}
```

With the above program:

- We are opening the file "Hello.html" with the 'FileMode.Open' and 'FileAccess.Read' options, so that we can read from the file.

- The variable 'bytes' is used to store all the bytes that are read from the file.

- The function 'System.Text.Encoding.UTF8.GetString' is used to convert the list of bytes into a string.

With this program, the output is as shown below. The output will vary depending on the contents of the source file.

Number of bytes in the file 73

<!DOCTYPE html>

<html>

<body>

<h1>Hello World</h1>

</body>

</html>

Let's now look at an example of how to use the FileStream class to write the contents to a file.

Example 11: The following program shows how to use the FileStream class to write contents to a file.

```
using System;
using System.IO;

namespace Demo
{
```

```
      class Program
   {

      // The main function
      static void Main(string[] args)
      {

         // Opening the file in read only mode
         FileStream src = new
FileStream(@"G:\newHello.txt",FileMode.Open, FileAccess.Write);

         string str="Hello World";

         // Converting the string to bytes to write
         byte[] bytes = new byte[str.Length];
         bytes = System.Text.Encoding.UTF8.GetBytes(str);

         // This will be used to store the number of bytes written to
the file
         int i = 0;

         src.Write(bytes,0,str.Length);
         Console.Read();
      }
   }
}
```

With the above program:

- We are opening the file "newHello.txt" with 'FileMode.Open' and 'FileAccess.Write', so that we can write contents to the file.

- The variable 'bytes' is used to store all the bytes that are going to be written to the file.

- The function 'System.Text.Encoding.UTF8.GetBytes' is used to convert the string to a list of bytes.

- These bytes are then written to the file using the 'Write' function

Now when we look at the newHello.txt file, we will see the text "Hello World" stored in the file.

3.5 StreamReader

This class can be used to read the contents from a stream, such as a file. The general syntax when creating a new object of this class is given below.

```
StreamReader fileobj = new StreamReader("nameoffile")
```

With this code, we just need to specify the name of the file. Once the file has been opened using the StreamReader class, we can use the built-in functions, such as ReadLine, to read the contents of the file line by line.

Let's look at an example of how to use the StreamReader class.

Example 12: The program below showcases the way to use the StreamReader class.

```
using System;
using System.IO;

namespace Demo
{
    class Program
    {
```

```
      // The main function
      static void Main(string[] args)
      {

          // Opening the file in read only mode
          StreamReader src = new
StreamReader(@"G:\newHello.html");

          // Displaying the first line of the file
          Console.WriteLine(src.ReadLine());
          Console.Read();
      }
   }
}
```

With this program, the output is as shown below. The output will vary depending on the contents of the source file.

Hello World

If we have many lines in the file, we can use the ReadtoEnd function to read all the contents of the file as shown in the example below.

Example 13: This program shows how to use the StreamReader class with the ReadtoEnd function.

```
using System;
using System.IO;

namespace Demo
{
    class Program
    {
```

```
    // The main function
    static void Main(string[] args)
    {

        // Opening the file in read only mode
        StreamReader src = new
StreamReader(@"G:\newHello.html");

        // Displaying all the contents of the file
        Console.WriteLine(src.ReadToEnd());
        Console.Read();
    }
  }
}
```

With this program, the output is as below. The output will again vary depending on the contents of the source file.

Hello World

Hello World Again

3.6 StreamWriter

This class can be used to write contents to a stream, such as a file. The general syntax when creating a new object of this class is given below.

```
StreamWriter fileobj = new StreamWriter("nameoffile")
```

With this code, we only need to specify the name of the file. Once the file has been opened using the StreamWriter class, we can use the built-in functions, such as Write and WriteLine, to write the contents to the file.

32

Let's look at an example of how to use the StreamReader class.

Example 14: The program below is used to show the way to use the StreamWriter class.

```
using System;
using System.IO;

namespace Demo
{
    class Program
  {

    // The main function
    static void Main(string[] args)
    {

      // Opening the file in append mode
      StreamWriter src = new
StreamWriter(@"G:\newHello.html");

      // Writing contents to the file
      src.WriteLine("Hello World");
      Console.Read();
    }
  }
}
```

Now if we open the "newHello.html" file, we will have the string 'Hello World' in the file.

We can also ensure that whenever content is written to a file, it is appended to the end of the file. All we need to do is to add the keyword of 'true' when opening the file using the StreamWriter.

The example below shows how this can be done.

Example 15: The following program shows how to use the StreamWriter class to append data.

```
using System;
using System.IO;

namespace Demo
{
    class Program
    {

    // The main function
    static void Main(string[] args)
    {

        // Opening the file in append mode
        StreamWriter src = new
StreamWriter(@"G:\newHello.html",true);

        // Writing contents to the file
        src.WriteLine("Hello World");
        Console.Read();
    }
    }
}
```

3.7 StringReader

StringReader enables you to read a string synchronously or asynchronously. The general syntax when creating a new object of this class is given below.

```
StringReader  obj = new StringReader  (stringvalue)
```

Let's look at an example of how to use the StringReader class.

Example 16: The next program shows the way to use the StringReader class.

```
using System;
using System.IO;

namespace Demo
{
    class Program
  {

    // The main function
    static void Main(string[] args)
    {

    // Building the string
    System.Text.StringBuilder stringToRead = new
System.Text.StringBuilder();
    stringToRead.AppendLine("Hello");
    stringToRead.AppendLine("World");
    stringToRead.AppendLine("again");

    // Using String Reader
    StringReader reader = new
StringReader(stringToRead.ToString());

    // Reading a line from the string
    string txt = reader.ReadLine();
    Console.WriteLine(txt);
    Console.Read();
    }
  }
}
```

In the above program we are:

• First building a string using the 'StringBuilder' class.

- Then we create a new 'StringReader' object using the 'StringBuilder' object as the source.

- Lastly, we use the 'ReadLine' function to read a line from the string.

With this program, the output is as follows:

Hello

We can also use the StringReader class to read all the contents of a string using the ReadtoEnd function as shown below.

Example 17: The program below shows how to use the StringReader class with the ReadtoEnd function.

```
using System;
using System.IO;
namespace Demo
{
    class Program
  {
    // The main function
    static void Main(string[] args)
    {

      // Building the string
      System.Text.StringBuilder stringToRead = new
System.Text.StringBuilder();
      stringToRead.AppendLine("Hello");
      stringToRead.AppendLine("World");
      stringToRead.AppendLine("again");

      // Using String Reader
      StringReader reader = new
StringReader(stringToRead.ToString());
```

```
        // Reading a line from the string
        string txt = reader.ReadToEnd();
        Console.WriteLine(txt);
        Console.Read();
      }
    }
}
```

With this program, the output is as follows:

Hello

World

again

3.8 StringWriter

StringWriter enables you to write a string synchronously or asynchronously. The general syntax when creating a new object of this class is given below.

```
StringWriter  obj = new StringReader  (StringWriter)
```

Let's look at an example of how to use the StringWriter class.

Example 18: This program showcases the way to use the StringWriter class.

```
using System;
using System.IO;

namespace Demo
{
    class Program
```

```
{

    // The main function
    static void Main(string[] args)
    {

        // Using String writer
        StringWriter strWriter = new StringWriter();

        // Writing strings to StringWriter

        strWriter.WriteLine("Hello");
        strWriter.WriteLine("World");
        strWriter.WriteLine("Again");

        // Writing the string to the console
        Console.WriteLine(strWriter.ToString());
        Console.Read();
    }
  }
}
```

With this program, the output is as follows:

Hello

World

again

4. Exception Handling

Not all programs that we develop can be completely foolproof, which means that errors can pop up when a program is being used. Commonly, users can enter the wrong input which leads to an error in the program.

Normally when an error occurs, the program could terminate. This leads to a bad user experience. In fact, it would have been better if the program could have taken care of the error and proceeded ahead, so that functionality wasn't affected.

This is where exception handling comes in. Exception handling is the ability of the program to catch errors or exceptions, take care of them, and proceed ahead with the normal running of the program.

Exceptions are implemented by using the statements below:

- try - A try block identifies a block of code in which the exception can occur. We place the block of code in the try block.

- catch - This block is used to handle the exception if it occurs.

- finally - The finally block is used to execute a given set of statements, whether an exception is thrown or not.

The syntax for using the above statements is shown below.

```
try
{
  //Code block that can cause the exception
}
catch( ExceptionName e1 )
{
  // error handling code
}
finally
{
  // statements to be executed
}
```

Now let's look at a simple example of using the try catch block.

Example 19: The following program is used to showcase the way to use the exception handling blocks.

```
using System;
using System.IO;

namespace Demo
{
    class Program
  {

    // The main function
    static void Main(string[] args)
    {

      int[] i = new int[2];
      // Placing the code in the try block
      try
      {
        // We are placing invalid code
```

```
            i[3] = 3;
        }
        // Here is where we catch the exception and display the
error message
        catch(Exception ex)
        {
            Console.WriteLine(ex.Message);
        }
            Console.Read();
        }
    }
}
```

With the above program we are:

- Creating a 'try, catch' block.

- In the 'try' block we are performing an illegal operation. Ideally the array only has 2 values, but we are trying to access a value that cannot be defined in the array.

- If we did not have the 'try, catch' block, the code would just terminate. But in our case, the 'catch' block will get the error and display it in the console.

With this program, the output is as follows:

Index was outside the bounds of the array

4.1 Built-in Exceptions

We can also use the built-in exceptions available in C# to catch errors. The table of available exception is shown below.

Table 2: Exceptions

Exception	Description
System.IO.IOException	This is used to handle I/O errors
System.IndexOutOfRangeException	This is used to handle errors generated when a method refers to an array index out of range
System.ArrayTypeMismatchException	This is used to handle errors generated when the type is mismatched with the array type
System.NullReferenceException	This is used to handle errors generated from referencing a null object
System.DivideByZeroException	This is used to handle errors generated from dividing a dividend with zero
System.InvalidCastException	This is used to handle errors generated during typecasting
System.OutOfMemoryException	This is used to handle errors generated from insufficient free memory
System.StackOverflowException	This is used to handle errors generated from stack overflow

This means we could have written our earlier program in the following way.

Example 20: The following program shows how to use the built-in exceptions.

```csharp
using System;
using System.IO;

namespace Demo
{
    class Program
    {

        // The main function
        static void Main(string[] args)
        {

            int[] i = new int[2];
            // Placing the code in the try block
            try
            {
                // We are placing invalid code
                i[3] = 3;
            }
            // Here is where we catch the exception and display the
error message
            catch (System.IndexOutOfRangeException ex)
            {
                Console.WriteLine(ex.Message);
            }
            Console.Read();
        }
    }
}
```

With this program, the output is as follows:

Index was outside the bounds of the array

We can also use multiple catch blocks. The catch blocks would be evaluated in sequential order to determine which would be the best fit. An example is shown below.

Example 21: The program below showcases the way to use multiple catch blocks.

```
using System;
using System.IO;
namespace Demo
{
    class Program
    {
    // The main function
    static void Main(string[] args)
    {
      int[] i = new int[2];
      // Placing the code in the try block
      try
      {
        // We are placing invalid code
        i[3] = 3;
      }
      // Here is where we catch the exception and display the error
message
      catch (System.IO.IOException ex1)
      {
        Console.WriteLine(ex1.Message);
      }
      catch (System.IndexOutOfRangeException ex)
      {
        Console.WriteLine(ex.Message);
      }
        Console.Read();
    }
  }
}
```

With this program, the output is as follows:

Index was outside the bounds of the array

5. Attributes

Attributes are used to add additional information to C# code. For example, we can add attribute information to a class which helps describe the class.

The general syntax of the attribute declaration is shown below.

```
[AttributeUsage(AttributeTargets.All)]
public class AttributeName : System.Attribute
{
//Define positional parameters
//Define named parameters

//constructor
}
```

The following things need to be noted:

- The 'Attribute' class is derived from the 'System.Attribute' class.

- The attribute 'AttributeUsage' specifies the language elements to which the attribute can be applied.

- The class needs to have a constructor definition.

Attribute classes have two types of parameters. The first is positional parameters, which must be specified every time the attribute is used. Positional parameters are specified as constructor arguments to the attribute class. The second type of parameter is named parameters, which are optional. If they are specified when the attribute is used, the name of the parameter must be used.

Attribute parameters are restricted to constant values of the following types:

- Simple types (bool, byte, char, short, int, long, float, and double)

- String

- System.Type

- Enums

- Object

- One-dimensional arrays of any of the above types

Now let's look at an example on the usage of attributes.

Example 22: The following program is used to show the way to use attributes in C#.

```
using System;
using System.IO;

namespace Demo
{
  [AttributeUsage(AttributeTargets.All)]
  public class TypeAttribute : System.Attribute
  {
    public readonly string Type;
    public string Subject        // Topic is a named parameter
    {
```

```csharp
        get
        {
            return Subject;
        }
        set
        {

            Subject = value;
        }
    }

    public TypeAttribute(string type)  // type is a positional
parameter
    {
        this.Type = type;
    }
}
[TypeAttribute("Student")]
class Person
{
    public int ID;
    public string name;

    void Display()
    {
        Console.WriteLine("The ID of the student is " + ID);
        Console.WriteLine("The Name of the student is " + name);
    }
}

    class Program
{
    // The main function
    static void Main(string[] args)
}
}
```

In the above program:

- We are defining an attribute class called 'TypeAttribute', which can be applied to any C# code.

- We then define a positional and named parameter.

- We also associate the attribute with a class, and state that the 'Person' class will contain the information pertinent to 'Students'.

- Lastly we use the 'System.Reflection' method to get the attribute information of the class and display it accordingly.

With this program, the output is as follows:

Demo.TypeAttribute

Now let's look at another example on the usage of an attribute. This time around, we are going to do two things. First we are going to use constructors to provide a value to a custom attribute, and then we are going to get the value of the custom attribute.

Example 23: The following program showcases another way to use attributes in C#.

```
using System;
using System.Reflection;
namespace Demo
{
    public class CustomAttribute : Attribute
    {
        // Private fields.
        private string name;
```

```csharp
      public CustomAttribute(string name)
      {
         this.name = name;
      }

      // Define Name property.
      // This is a read-only attribute.

      public virtual string Name
      {
         get { return name; }
      }
   }

   [Custom("John")]
   class Person
   {
      public int ID;
      public string name;

      void Display()
      {
         Console.WriteLine("The ID of the student is " + ID);
         Console.WriteLine("The Name of the student is " + name);
      }
   }

   class Program
   {
      static void Main(string[] args)
      {

         Type t = typeof(Person);
         CustomAttribute MyAttribute =
         (CustomAttribute)Attribute.GetCustomAttribute(t,
typeof(CustomAttribute));
```

```
        if (MyAttribute == null)
        {
            Console.WriteLine("The attribute was not found.");
        }
        else
        {
            // Get the Name value.
            Console.WriteLine("The Name Attribute is " +
MyAttribute.Name);
        }
        Console.ReadKey();
        }
    }
}
```

In the above program:

- We are defining a constructor, so that when assigning a value to the attribute, it is assigned to the 'Name' property.

- In the main program, we first get the class type. Then we use that type, along with the reflection of the 'Custom' attribute class, to get the value of the 'Name' property.

With this program, the output is as follows:

The Name Attribute is John

6. Properties

Properties are members of a class that can be accessed using 'getter' and 'setter' methods. This is normally used to get and set the values of private members of a class.

The syntax for defining a property is shown below.

```
public datatype propertyname
{
  get
  {
    return propertyname;
  }
  set
  {
    propertyname = value;
  }
}
```

Where:

- 'datatype' is the type of data associated with the property.

- 'propertyname' is the name of the property.

- The 'get' and 'set' methods are used to get and set the value of the property.

Before we jump into an example on properties, let's look at a classic example of how we would get and set fields of a typical class.

Example 24: The program below shows how to use fields in a class.

```
using System;
using System.IO;

namespace Demo
{

  class Student
  {
    private int ID;
    private string name;

    // Method used to input the value of ID and name
    public void Input(int pid, string pname)
    {
      ID = pid;
      name = pname;
    }

    // Method used to display the value of ID and name
    public void Display()
    {
      Console.WriteLine("The ID of the student is " + ID);
      Console.WriteLine("The Name of the student is " + name);
    }
  }

  class Program
  {
    // The main function
    static void Main(string[] args)
```

```
      {
          Student stud1 = new Student();
          stud1.Input(1, "John");
          stud1.Display();
          Console.Read();
      }
  }
}
```

In the above program:

- We are defining a method called 'Input', which is used to enter the value of 'ID' and the value of 'Name' into the object of the 'Student' class.

- Then we use the 'Display' function to display the value of the member's ID and Name.

With this program, the output is as follows:

The ID of the student is 1

The Name of the student is John

Now let's apply the concept of properties to see how the program changes.

Example 25: The next program is used to showcase how to use properties in a class.

```
using System;
using System.IO;

namespace Demo
{

    class Student
```

```
{
    // Defining the members
    private int id;
    private string name;

    // Defining the properties
    public int ID
    {
        get
        {
            return id;
        }
        set
        {
            id = value;
        }
    }

    public string Name
    {
        get
        {
            return name;
        }
        set
        {
            name = value;
        }
    }
}

class Program
{
    // The main function
    static void Main(string[] args)
    {
```

```
        Student stud1 = new Student();
        stud1.ID = 1;
        stud1.Name = "John";

        Console.WriteLine("The ID of the student is " + stud1.ID);
        Console.WriteLine("The Name of the student is " +
stud1.Name);
        Console.Read();
    }
  }
}
```

In this program we have:

- Separate getter and setter properties for 'ID' and 'Name'. They map to the private members of ID and Name.

- We can then access these members from any class.

With this program, the output is as follows:

The ID of the student is 1

The Name of the student is John

6.1 Properties in Abstract Classes

If you have properties in abstract classes, then the implementation of those properties should be present in the derived class.

To illustrate, we can have an abstract class as shown below.

```
public abstract class Person
{
```

```
      public abstract int ID
      {
        get;
        set;
      }
      public abstract string Name
      {
        get;
        set;
      }
  }
```

This class has plain get and set methods, with the properties
defined as 'abstract'. Next, in order to ensure that the derived
class uses these properties, we need to mention the 'override'
keyword with the property.

```
class Student : Person
  {
    // Defining the members
    private int id;
    private string name;

    // Defining the properties
    public override int ID
    {
      get
      {
        return id;
      }
      set
      {
        id = value;
      }
    }
```

```
public override string Name
{
  get
  {
    return name;
  }
  set
  {
    name = value;
  }
}
}
```

Let's look at a complete example of how to implement everything together.

Example 26: The following program shows the way to use properties in an abstract class.

```
using System;
using System.IO;
namespace Demo
{
  public abstract class Person
  {
    public abstract int ID
    {
      get;
      set;
    }
    public abstract string Name
    {
      get;
      set;
    }
```

```csharp
}
class Student : Person
{
    // Defining the members
    private int id;
    private string name;

    // Defining the properties
    public override int ID
    {
        get
        {
            return id;
        }
        set
        {
            id = value;
        }
    }

    public override string Name
    {
        get
        {
            return name;
        }
        set
        {
            name = value;
        }
    }
}

    class Program
{
    // The main function
    static void Main(string[] args)
```

```
    {
        Student stud1 = new Student();
        stud1.ID = 1;
        stud1.Name = "John";

        Console.WriteLine("The ID of the student is " + stud1.ID);
        Console.WriteLine("The Name of the student is " +
stud1.Name);
        Console.Read();
    }
  }
}
```

With this program, the output is as follows:

The ID of the student is 1

The Name of the student is John

6.2 Read Only Properties

If we want a property to only be a read-only property, then we need to ensure that the 'setter' is not present for that property.

In the example below, if we didn't want to be able to set the 'Name' property, we would simply omit the setter property.

```
    public string Name
    {
      get
      {
        return name;
      }
    }
```

Let's look at a complete example of this.

Example 27: The program below showcases how to use read only properties.

```
using System;
using System.IO;

namespace Demo
{

  class Student
  {
    // Defining the members
    private int id;
    private string name;
    private int subjectID = 1;

    // Defining a read only property
    public int SubjectID
    {
      get
      {
        return subjectID;
      }
    }
    public int ID
    {
      get
      {
        return id;
      }
      set
      {
        id = value;
      }
    }
```

```csharp
        public string Name
        {
            get
            {
                return name;
            }
            set
            {
                name = value;
            }
        }
    }

    class Program
    {
        // The main function
        static void Main(string[] args)
        {

            Student stud1 = new Student();
            stud1.ID = 1;
            stud1.Name = "John";

            Console.WriteLine("The ID of the student is " + stud1.ID);
            Console.WriteLine("The Name of the student is " +
stud1.Name);
            Console.WriteLine("The SubjectID is " + stud1.SubjectID);
            Console.Read();
        }
    }
}
```

Since we are defining the 'SubjectID' property with only the 'getter' property, we cannot set the value of the property.

With this program, the output is as follows:

The ID of the student is 1

The Name of the student is John

The SubjectID is 1

7. Delegates

Delegates are used in C# to create pointers to methods. The pointer can point to any method at any time. We can then call or invoke the method via the 'delegate' instance.

Delegates have the following properties:

- Delegates are type safe pointers.

- They allow methods to be passed as parameters.

- They can be used to define callback methods.

- They can be chained together.

The delegate is defined through the following steps:

- Define the method that will be attached to the delegate.

- Declare the delegate itself. An example is shown below.

```
public delegate void Del();
```

- Create a variable of the delegate and assign the method to the delegate.

- Call the method via the delegate.

Let's now look at an example of how to structure the above steps.

Example 28: The following program is used to showcase the way to use a delegate.

```
using System;
using System.IO;

namespace Demo
{
  class Program
  {
    // This is the method which will be pointed to by the delegate
function
    public static void Display()
    {
      Console.WriteLine("Hello world");
    }

    // Defining the delegate
    public delegate void Del();
    // The main function
    static void Main(string[] args)
    {

      //Assigning the method to the delegate
      Del handler = Display;

      // Calling the method via the delegate
      handler();
      Console.Read();
    }
  }
}
```

With this program, the output is as follows:

Hello World

Let's now look at an example of how to use a delegate with multiple methods.

Example 29: The next program shows how to use a delegate with multiple methods.

```
using System;
using System.IO;

namespace Demo
{
  class Program
  {
    // This is the method which will be pointed to by the delegate
function
    public static void DisplayA()
    {
      Console.WriteLine("Hello world");
    }

    public static void DisplayB()
    {
      Console.WriteLine("Hello world again");
    }

    // Defining the delegate
    public delegate void Del();
    // The main function
    static void Main(string[] args)
    {

      //Assigning the method to the delegate
      Del handler = DisplayA;
```

```
        // Calling the method via the delegate
        handler();

        //Assigning the method to the delegate
        handler = DisplayB;

        // Calling the method via the delegate
        handler();

        Console.Read();
    }
  }
}
```

With this program, the output is as follows:

Hello World

Hello World again

7.1 Delegates with Parameters

We can have methods that take in parameters, while also having delegates take in the same parameters. Let's look at an example of this.

Example 30: The following program showcases the way to use a delegate with parameters.

```
using System;
using System.IO;

namespace Demo
{
```

```csharp
class Program
{
    // This is the method which will be pointed to by the delegate
function
    public static void DisplayA(int i)
    {
        Console.WriteLine("The integer value is "+i);
    }

    public static void DisplayB(int j)
    {
        Console.WriteLine("The integer value is "+j);
    }

    // Defining the delegate
    public delegate void Del(int i);
    // The main function
    static void Main(string[] args)
    {
        //Assigning the method to the delegate
        Del handler = DisplayA;

        // Calling the method via the delegate
        handler(1);

        //Assigning the method to the delegate
        handler = DisplayB;

        // Calling the method via the delegate
        handler(2);

        Console.Read();
    }
}
}
```

With this program, the output is as follows:

The integer value is 1

The integer value is 2

Delegates can also be applied to objects of a class. An example is shown below.

Example 31: This program showcases the way to use a delegate with class objects.

```
using System;
using System.IO;

namespace Demo
{
  class Student
  {
    // Defining the members
    private int id;
    private string name;
    private int subjectID = 1;

    // Defining a read only property
    public int SubjectID
    {
      get
      {
        return subjectID;
      }
    }

    public int ID
    {
      get
      {
        return id;
```

```csharp
        }
        set
        {
            id = value;
        }
    }

    public string Name
    {
        get
        {
            return name;
        }
        set
        {
            name = value;
        }
    }

    public void Display()
    {
        Console.WriteLine("The ID is " + id);
        Console.WriteLine("The name is " + name);
    }
}

class Program
{
    // Defining the delegate
    public delegate void Del();
    // The main function
    static void Main(string[] args)
    {
        Student stud1 = new Student();
        stud1.ID = 1;
        stud1.Name = "John";
```

```
        //Assigning the method to the delegate
        Del handler = stud1.Display;

        // Calling the method via the delegate
        handler();
        Console.Read();
      }
    }
}
```

With this program, the output is as follows:

The ID is 1

The name is John

8. Reflection

Reflection is the ability in C# to get information of a particular piece of code at runtime. For example if we wanted to find out more information on a method, we could use reflection. By using reflection in C#, one is able to find out details of an object or method, as well as create objects and invoke methods at runtime.

Let's look at a simple example of how we can achieve this. In this example, we are going to use the 'Type' datatype, which can be used to extract information about a particular class.

Example 32: The following program shows how to use Type to get information on a class

```
using System;
using System.IO;

namespace Demo
{
    class Student
    {
        // Defining the members
        public int id;
        public  string name;

        public void Display()
        {
```

```
        Console.WriteLine("The ID is " + id);
        Console.WriteLine("The name is " + name);
    }
}

class Program
{
    // The main function
    static void Main(string[] args)
    {
        Student stud1 = new Student();

        // Trying to get the type of object
        Type myTypeObj = stud1.GetType();

        Console.WriteLine("The object is of Type " + myTypeObj);
        Console.Read();
    }
}
}
```

In the above program we are:

- Using 'Type' to extract information about the 'stud1' object.

- Using this, we can extract the name of the class of the object.

With this program, the output is as follows:

The object is of Type Demo.Student

8.1 MethodInfo

This reflection method can be used to get information about a method within a class. Let's look at an example of this.

Example 33: The next program showcases the way to use MethodInfo.

```
using System;
using System.IO;
using System.Reflection;

namespace Demo
{
    class Student
    {
        // Defining the members
        public int id;
        public  string name;

        public void Display()
        {
            Console.WriteLine("The ID is " + id);
            Console.WriteLine("The name is " + name);
        }
    }

    class Program
    {
        // The main function
        static void Main(string[] args)
        {

            Student stud1 = new Student();

            // Trying to get the type of object
            Type myTypeObj = stud1.GetType();
```

```
        Console.WriteLine("The object is of Type " + myTypeObj);

        // Using reflection to get information about the Display
method
        MethodInfo myMethodInfo =
myTypeObj.GetMethod("Display");

        Console.WriteLine("Is the method a static method " +
myMethodInfo.IsStatic);
        Console.Read();
      }
    }
}
```

With this program, the output is as follows:

The object is of Type Demo.Student

Is the method a static method False

9. Collections

Collections are special classes in C# that can make working with special data classes considerably easier.

For example, instead of writing special code to find out the size of an array, we can use the built-in function of the arrayList collection, called size(), to get the size of the array. Hence, collections are specialized classes that can be used in C# programs.

The collections below are present in C#:

- ArrayList - The array container is used to store a contiguous set of values of the same data type.

- SortedList - Lists are sequence containers that allow constant time insert and erase operations anywhere within the sequence, and iteration in both directions.

- Stacks - This is a type of collection specifically designed to operate in a LIFO (last-in first-out) context, where elements are inserted and extracted only from one end of the container.

- Queues - This is a type of collection specifically designed to operate in a FIFO (first-in first-out) context, where elements are inserted into one end of the container and extracted from the other.

Let's look at each collection in more detail.

9.1 ArrayList

The arrayList container is used to store a contiguous set of values of the same data type. Let's look at the definition of an array container via a sample code.

The syntax for defining an array container is as follows:

```
ArrayList variablename=new ArrayList():
```

In this code, 'variablename' refers to the variable name that is to be assigned to the array list. To add an element to the array list, we use the 'Add()' method as shown below.

```
Variablename.Add(element)
```

Here, 'element' refers to the value that needs to be added to the array list. To view the element, we can simply reference it via the index number. Let's now look at an example on how to use the ArrayList collection.

Example 34: The following program is used to show the way to use array lists.

```
using System;
using System.Collections;

namespace Demo
{
    class Program
    {
        // The main function
        static void Main(string[] args)
        {
            // Defining the ArrayList
            ArrayList ar = new ArrayList();
```

```
      // Adding elements to the array list
      ar.Add(1);
      ar.Add(2);
      ar.Add(3);

      // Displaying the elements of the array
      Console.WriteLine(" The first element of the array is " +
ar[0]);
      Console.WriteLine(" The second element of the array is " +
ar[1]);
      Console.WriteLine(" The third element of the array is " +
ar[2]);

      Console.Read();
    }
  }
}
```

With this program, the output is as follows:

The first element of the array is 1

The second element of the array is 2

The third element of the array is 3

We can add any type of data type to the array list. Let's look at an example of an ArrayList of Strings.

Example 35: This program shows the way to use array lists of strings.

```
using System;
using System.Collections;

namespace Demo
{
  class Program
```

```
{
    // The main function
    static void Main(string[] args)
    {
        // Defining the ArrayList
        ArrayList ar = new ArrayList();

        // Adding elements to the array list
        ar.Add("Hello");
        ar.Add("World");
        ar.Add("Again");

        // Displaying the elements of the array
        Console.WriteLine(" The first element of the array is " +
ar[0]);
        Console.WriteLine(" The second element of the array is " +
ar[1]);
        Console.WriteLine(" The third element of the array is " +
ar[2]);

        Console.Read();
    }
}
}
```

With this program, the output is as follows:

The first element of the array is Hello

The second element of the array is World

The third element of the array is Again

The ArrayList class has a variety of operations that can be performed. Let's look at each one of these operations in more detail.

9.2 ArrayList Operations

The section below summarizes the various operations available for ArrayList.

Table 3: ArrayList Operations

Function	Description
size	This property is used to get the size of the ArrayList
Clear()	This function is used to clear the elements of the ArrayList
Contains()	This function is used to check if the ArrayList contains a particular value. The function returns a True value if the ArrayList contain the value else it will return False
IndexOf()	This function is used to give the index of a particular value in the ArrayList
InsertAt()	This function is used to insert a value at a particular position in the ArrayList
Remove()	This function is used to remove a value from the ArrayList
RemoveAt()	This function is used to remove a value at a particular position from the ArrayList
Reverse()	This function is used to reverse the elements in an ArrayList
Sort()	This function is used to sort the elements in an ArrayList

Function	Description
GetRange()	This function is used to get a range of elements and assign it to another Array List

Now let's look at each function individually and how they work.

9.2.1 Size Function

This property is used to get the size of the ArrayList.

Example 36: The following program shows how to use count property.

```
using System;
using System.Collections;

namespace Demo
{
  class Program
  {
    // The main function
    static void Main(string[] args)
    {
      // Defining the ArrayList
      ArrayList ar = new ArrayList();

      // Adding elements to the array list
      ar.Add(1);
      ar.Add(2);
      ar.Add(3);
```

```
// Displaying the size of the array list
Console.WriteLine(" The size of the array list is " + ar.Count);

        Console.Read();
    }
  }
}
```

With this program, the output is as follows:

The size of the array list is 3

9.2.2 Clear Function

This function is used to clear the elements of the ArrayList.

Example 37: The following program showcases the way to use clear method.

```
using System;
using System.Collections;
namespace Demo
{
  class Program
  {
    // The main function
    static void Main(string[] args)
    {
      // Defining the ArrayList
      ArrayList ar = new ArrayList();

      // Adding elements to the array list
      ar.Add(1);
      ar.Add(2);
      ar.Add(3);
```

```
        // Clearing all the elements of the array list
        ar.Clear();

        Console.WriteLine(" The size of the array list is " + ar.Count);
        Console.Read();
      }
    }
}
```

With this program, the output is as follows:

The size of the array list is 0

9.2.3 Contains Function

This function is used to check if the ArrayList contains a particular value. The function returns a true value if the ArrayList contains the value, else it will return a false value.

Example 38: The next program shows how to use the contains method.

```
using System;
using System.Collections;

namespace Demo
{
  class Program
  {
    // The main function
    static void Main(string[] args)
    {
      // Defining the ArrayList
      ArrayList ar = new ArrayList();
```

```
        // Adding elements to the array list
        ar.Add(1);
        ar.Add(2);
        ar.Add(3);

        Console.WriteLine("Does the array contain the value 3 " +
ar.Contains(3));
        Console.Read();
      }
    }
}
```

With this program, the output is as follows:

Does the array contain the value 3 True

9.2.4 IndexOf Function

This function is used to obtain the index of a particular value in the ArrayList.

Example 39: The following program is used to show the way to use the IndexOf method.

```
using System;
using System.Collections;

namespace Demo
{
  class Program
  {
    // The main function
    static void Main(string[] args)
    {
```

```
        // Defining the ArrayList
        ArrayList ar = new ArrayList();

        // Adding elements to the array list
        ar.Add(1);
        ar.Add(2);
        ar.Add(3);

        Console.WriteLine("The index of value 3 is  " +
ar.IndexOf(3));
        Console.Read();
      }
   }
}
```

With this program, the output is as follows:

The index of value 3 is 2

9.2.5 Insert Function

This function is used to insert a value at a particular position in the ArrayList.

Example 40: The program below showcases the insert method.

```
using System;
using System.Collections;
namespace Demo
{
   class Program
   {
      // The main function
      static void Main(string[] args)
```

```
    {
        // Defining the ArrayList
        ArrayList ar = new ArrayList();

        // Adding elements to the array list
        ar.Add(1);
        ar.Add(2);
        ar.Add(3);

        Console.WriteLine("The index of value 3 is  " +
ar.IndexOf(3));

        // Inserting the value 4 at Index position 2
        ar.Insert(2, 4);

        Console.WriteLine("The index of value 3 is  " +
ar.IndexOf(3));
        Console.Read();
    }
  }
}
```

With this program, the output is as follows:

The index of value 3 is 3

The index of value 3 is 3

9.2.6 Remove Function

This function is used to remove a value from the ArrayList.

Example 41: The following program is used to showcase the way to use the remove method.

```
using System;
using System.Collections;

namespace Demo
{
    class Program
    {
        // The main function
        static void Main(string[] args)
        {
            // Defining the ArrayList
            ArrayList ar = new ArrayList();

            // Adding elements to the array list
            ar.Add(1);
            ar.Add(2);
            ar.Add(3);

            Console.WriteLine("The value at position 1 is  " + ar[1]);

            // Removing a value
            ar.Remove(2);

            Console.WriteLine("The value at position 1 is  " + ar[1]);
            Console.Read();
        }
    }
}
```

With this program, the output is as follows:

The value at position 1 is 2

The value at position 1 is 3

9.2.7 RemoveAt Function

This function is used to remove a value at a particular position from the ArrayList.

Example 42: This program shows the way to use the RemoveAt method.

```
using System;
using System.Collections;

namespace Demo
{
    class Program
    {
        // The main function
        static void Main(string[] args)
        {
            // Defining the ArrayList
            ArrayList ar = new ArrayList();

            // Adding elements to the array list
            ar.Add(1);
            ar.Add(2);
            ar.Add(3);

            Console.WriteLine("The value at position 1 is  " + ar[1]);

            // Removing a value
            ar.RemoveAt(1);

            Console.WriteLine("The value at position 1 is  " + ar[1]);
            Console.Read();
        }
    }
}
```

With this program, the output is as follows:

The value at position 1 is 2

The value at position 1 is 3

9.2.8 Reverse Function

This function is used to reverse the elements in an ArrayList.

Example 43: The following program showcases the reverse method.

```
using System;
using System.Collections;
namespace Demo
{
   class Program
   {
      // The main function
      static void Main(string[] args)
      {
         // Defining the ArrayList
         ArrayList ar = new ArrayList();

         // Adding elements to the array list
         ar.Add(1);
         ar.Add(2);
         ar.Add(3);

         Console.WriteLine("The value at position 0 is " + ar[0]);
         Console.WriteLine("The value at position 1 is " + ar[1]);
         Console.WriteLine("The value at position 2 is " + ar[2]);

         // Reversing the list
         ar.Reverse();
```

```
            Console.WriteLine("The value at position 0 is  " + ar[0]);
            Console.WriteLine("The value at position 1 is  " + ar[1]);
            Console.WriteLine("The value at position 2 is  " + ar[2]);

            Console.Read();
        }
    }
}
```

With this program, the output is as follows:

The value at position 0 is 1

The value at position 1 is 2

The value at position 2 is 3

The value at position 0 is 3

The value at position 1 is 2

The value at position 2 is 1

9.2.9 Sort Function

This function is used to sort the elements in an ArrayList.

Example 44: The program below is used to showcase the way to use the sort method.

```
using System;
using System.Collections;
namespace Demo
{
    class Program
    {
        // The main function
        static void Main(string[] args)
```

```
    {
        // Defining the ArrayList
        ArrayList ar = new ArrayList();

        // Adding elements to the array list
        ar.Add(3);
        ar.Add(2);
        ar.Add(1);

        Console.WriteLine("The value at position 0 is  " + ar[0]);
        Console.WriteLine("The value at position 1 is  " + ar[1]);
        Console.WriteLine("The value at position 2 is  " + ar[2]);

        // Sorting the list
        ar.Sort();

        Console.WriteLine("The value at position 0 is  " + ar[0]);
        Console.WriteLine("The value at position 1 is  " + ar[1]);
        Console.WriteLine("The value at position 2 is  " + ar[2]);

        Console.Read();
    }
  }
}
```

With this program, the output is as follows:

The value at position 0 is 3

The value at position 1 is 2

The value at position 2 is 1

The value at position 0 is 1

The value at position 1 is 2

The value at position 2 is 3

9.2.10 GetRange Function

This function is used to extract a range of elements from an ArrayList and assign it to another ArrayList.

Example 45: The following program shows how to use the GetRange method.

```
using System;
using System.Collections;

namespace Demo
{
    class Program
    {
        // The main function
        static void Main(string[] args)
        {
            // Defining the ArrayList
            ArrayList ar = new ArrayList();

            // Adding elements to the array list
            ar.Add(1);
            ar.Add(2);
            ar.Add(3);
            ar.Add(4);

            // Creating the new arraylist
            ArrayList ar1 = new ArrayList();
            ar1 = ar.GetRange(0, 2);

            Console.WriteLine("The value at position 0 is " + ar1[0]);
            Console.WriteLine("The value at position 1 is " + ar1[1]);
            Console.Read();
        }
    }
}
```

With this program, the output is as follows:

The value at position 0 is 1

The value at position 1 is 2

9.3 Stack

The stack collection is used to define a last-in-first-out collection. The syntax for defining a stack container is as follows:

```
Stack variablename=new Stack ():
```

In this code, 'variablename' is the variable name to be assigned to the stack. To add an element to the stack, we use the 'Push()' method as shown below.

```
Variablename.Push(element)
```

Here, 'element' is the value that needs to be added to the stack. Let's now look at an example of how to use the Stack collection.

Example 46: The following program showcases the way to use stacks.

```
using System;
using System.Collections;
namespace Demo
{
   class Program
   {
      // The main function
      static void Main(string[] args)
```

```
    {
        // Defining the Stack
        Stack ar = new Stack();

        // Adding elements to the Stack
        ar.Push(1);
        ar.Push(2);
        ar.Push(3);

        Console.Read();
    }
  }
}
```

The Stack class has a variety of operations that can be performed. Let's look at each one of these operations in more detail.

9.4 Stack Operations

The section below summarizes the details of the various operations available for stacks.

Table 4: Stack Operations

Function	Description
Count	This is used to get the number of elements on the stack
Clear	This is used to remove all the elements from the stack
Pop	This is used to pop an elements from the stack

Function	Description
Peek	This is used to see the top most element of the stack without removing the element
ToArray	This is used to output elements of the stack into an array
Contains	This is used to check if the stack contains a certain element

9.4.1 Count Function

This property is used to get the number of elements on the stack.

Example 47: The next program shows how to use the count property.

```
using System;
using System.Collections;

namespace Demo
{
  class Program
  {
    // The main function
    static void Main(string[] args)
    {
      // Defining the Stack
      Stack ar = new Stack();

      // Adding elements to the Stack
      ar.Push(1);
      ar.Push(2);
      ar.Push(3);
```

```
        Console.WriteLine("The number of elements on the stack is "
+ ar.Count);
        Console.Read();
      }
    }
}
```

With this program, the output is as follows:

The number of elements on the stack is 3

9.4.2 Clear Function

This function is used to remove all the elements from the stack.

Example 48: The following program showcases the clear function.

```
using System;
using System.Collections;
namespace Demo
{
  class Program
  {
    // The main function
    static void Main(string[] args)
    {
      // Defining the Stack
      Stack ar = new Stack();

      // Adding elements to the Stack
      ar.Push(1);
      ar.Push(2);
      ar.Push(3);
```

```
        Console.WriteLine("The number of elements on the stack is "
+ ar.Count);

        // Clearing the stack
        ar.Clear();

        Console.WriteLine("The number of elements on the stack is "
+ ar.Count);
        Console.Read();
      }
    }
}
```

With this program, the output is as follows:

The number of elements on the stack is 3

The number of elements on the stack is 0

9.4.3 Pop Function

This function is used to pop an element from the stack.

Example 49: The program below is used to showcase the way to use the pop function.

```
using System;
using System.Collections;

namespace Demo
{
  class Program
  {
    // The main function
    static void Main(string[] args)
    {
```

```
      // Defining the Stack
      Stack ar = new Stack();

      // Adding elements to the Stack
      ar.Push(1);
      ar.Push(2);
      ar.Push(3);

      Console.WriteLine("Popping an element from the stack " +
ar.Pop());
      Console.WriteLine("Popping an element from the stack " +
ar.Pop());
      Console.Read();
    }
  }
}
```

With this program, the output is as follows:

Popping an element from the stack 3

Popping an element from the stack 2

9.4.4 Peek Function

This function is used to view the top-most element on the stack without removing the element.

Example 50: The following program is used to show how to use the peek function.

```
using System;
using System.Collections;

namespace Demo
```

```
{
  class Program
  {
    // The main function
    static void Main(string[] args)
    {
      // Defining the Stack
      Stack ar = new Stack();

      // Adding elements to the Stack
      ar.Push(1);
      ar.Push(2);
      ar.Push(3);

      Console.WriteLine("The element at the top of the stack is " +
ar.Peek());
      Console.Read();
    }
  }
}
```

With this program, the output is as follows:

The element at the top of the stack is 3

9.4.5 ToArray Function

This function is used to output elements of the stack into an array.

Example 51: The next program shows the way to use the ToArray function.

```
using System;
using System.Collections;
```

```
namespace Demo
{
    class Program
    {
        // The main function
        static void Main(string[] args)
        {
            // Defining the Stack
            Stack ar = new Stack();
            object[] ar1 = new object[3];

            // Adding elements to the Stack
            ar.Push(1);
            ar.Push(2);
            ar.Push(3);

            // Transfering the elements to an array
            ar1=ar.ToArray();

            Console.WriteLine("The first element is " +
ar1[0].ToString());
            Console.WriteLine("The second element is " +
ar1[1].ToString());
            Console.WriteLine("The third element is " +
ar1[2].ToString());

            Console.Read();
        }
    }
}
```

With this program, the output is as follows:

The first element is 3

The second element is 2

The third element is 1

9.4.6 Contains Function

This function is used to check whether the stack contains a specified element.

Example 52: This program is used to showcase the contains function.

```
using System;
using System.Collections;

namespace Demo
{
  class Program
  {
    // The main function
    static void Main(string[] args)
    {
      // Defining the Stack
      Stack ar = new Stack();

      // Adding elements to the Stack
      ar.Push(1);
      ar.Push(2);
      ar.Push(3);

      // Transfering the elements to an array
      Console.WriteLine("Does the stack contain the element 2 " +
ar.Contains(3));
      Console.Read();
    }
  }
}
```

With this program, the output is as follows:

Does the stack contain the element 2 True

9.5 Queue

The Queue collection is used to define a first-in-first-out collection. The syntax for defining a Queue container is as follows:

```
Queue variablename=new Queue ():
```

In this code, 'variablename' is the variable name to be assigned to the Queue. To add an element to the Queue, we use the 'Enqueue()' method as shown below.

```
Variablename.Enqueue (element)
```

Here, 'element' is the value that needs to be added to the Queue. Let's now look at an example of how to use the Queue collection.

Example 53: The following program is used to showcase the way to use queues.

```csharp
using System;
using System.Collections;

namespace Demo
{
    class Program
    {
        // The main function
        static void Main(string[] args)
        {
            // Defining the Queue
            Queue ar = new Queue();

            // Adding elements to the Queue
            ar.Enqueue(1);
```

```
      ar.Enqueue(2);
      ar.Enqueue(3);

      Console.Read();
    }
  }
}
```

The Queue class has a variety of operations that can be performed. Let's look at each one of these operations in more detail.

9.6 Queue Operations

The section below shows the details of the various operations available for queues.

Table 5: Queue Operations

Function	Description
Count	This is used to get the number of elements in the queue
Clear	This is used to remove all the elements from the queue
ToArray	This is used to output the elements of the queue into an array
Dequeue	This is used to remove elements from the queue
Contains	This is used to check if the queue contains a certain element

9.6.1 Count Property

This property is used to get the number of elements in the queue.

Example 54: The program below is used to showcase the count property.

```
using System;
using System.Collections;

namespace Demo
{
  class Program
  {
    // The main function
    static void Main(string[] args)
    {
      // Defining the Queue
      Queue ar = new Queue();

      // Adding elements to the Queue
      ar.Enqueue(1);
      ar.Enqueue(2);
      ar.Enqueue(3);

      Console.WriteLine("The number of elements in the queue is "
+ ar.Count);
      Console.Read();
    }
  }
}
```

With this program, the output is as follows:

The number of elements in the queue is 3

9.6.2 DeQueue Function

This function is used to remove elements from the queue.

Example 55: The following program shows how to use the DeQueue function.

```
using System;
using System.Collections;

namespace Demo
{
  class Program
  {
    // The main function
    static void Main(string[] args)
    {
      // Defining the Queue
      Queue ar = new Queue();

      // Adding elements to the Queue
      ar.Enqueue(1);
      ar.Enqueue(2);
      ar.Enqueue(3);

      Console.WriteLine("The first element out of the queue is " +
ar.Dequeue());
      Console.WriteLine("The second element out of the queue is "
+ ar.Dequeue());
      Console.WriteLine("The third element out of the queue is " +
ar.Dequeue());

      Console.Read();
    }
  }
}
```

With this program, the output is as follows:

The first element out of the queue is 1

The second element out of the queue is 2

The third element out of the queue is 3

9.6.3 Clear Function

This function is used to clear elements from the queue.

Example 56: The following program is used to showcase the way to use the clear function.

```
using System;
using System.Collections;

namespace Demo
{
    class Program
    {
        // The main function
        static void Main(string[] args)
        {
            // Defining the Queue
            Queue ar = new Queue();

            // Adding elements to the Queue
            ar.Enqueue(1);
            ar.Enqueue(2);
            ar.Enqueue(3);

            Console.WriteLine("The number of elements in the queue is "
+ ar.Count);
```

```
      // Clearing the queue
      ar.Clear();
      Console.WriteLine("The number of elements in the queue is "
+ ar.Count);
      Console.Read();
    }
  }
}
```

With this program, the output is as follows:

The number of elements in the queue is 3

The number of elements in the queue is 0

9.6.4 Contains Function

This function is used to check whether the queue contains a particular element.

Example 57: The program below is used to showcase the contains function.

```
using System;
using System.Collections;

namespace Demo
{
  class Program
  {
    // The main function
    static void Main(string[] args)
    {
      // Defining the Queue
      Queue ar = new Queue();
```

```
        // Adding elements to the Queue
        ar.Enqueue(1);
        ar.Enqueue(2);
        ar.Enqueue(3);

        Console.WriteLine("Does the queue contain the element 2 " +
ar.Contains(2));
        Console.Read();
      }
    }
}
```

With this program, the output is as follows:

Does the queue contain the element 2 True

9.6.5 ToArray Function

This function is used to copy all the elements of the queue to an Array.

Example 58: The following program shows how to use the ToArray function.

```
using System;
using System.Collections;

namespace Demo
{
  class Program
  {
    // The main function
    static void Main(string[] args)
    {
```

```
        // Defining the Queue
        Queue ar = new Queue();
        Object[] ar1 = new Object[3];

        // Adding elements to the Queue
        ar.Enqueue(1);
        ar.Enqueue(2);
        ar.Enqueue(3);

        ar1 = ar.ToArray();

        Console.WriteLine("The first element of the array is " +
ar1[0].ToString());
        Console.WriteLine("The second element of the array is " +
ar1[1].ToString());
        Console.WriteLine("The third element of the array is " +
ar1[2].ToString());

        Console.Read();
     }
   }
}
```

With this program, the output is as follows:

The first element of the array is 1

The second element of the array is 2

The third element of the array is 3

9.7 SortedList

The SortedList collection is used to define a sorted list of elements that can be accessed via a key or index. The syntax for defining a SortedList container is as follows:

```
SortedList variablename=new SortedList ():
```

Where 'variablename' is the variable name to be assigned to the sorted list. To add an element to the sorted list, we use the 'Add()' method as shown below.

```
Variablename.Add (key,value)
```

Where each element consists of a key and a value. Let's now look at an example of how to use the SortedList collection.

Example 59: The next program is used to show the way to use SortedList.

```
using System;
using System.Collections;

namespace Demo
{
    class Program
    {
        // The main function
        static void Main(string[] args)
        {
            // Defining the SortedList
            SortedList ar = new SortedList();

            // Adding elements to the SortedList
            ar.Add(1,"One");
            ar.Add(2,"Two");
            ar.Add(3,"Three");

            // Displaying the values of each element in the SortedList
            Console.WriteLine("The first value of the SortedList is " +
ar[1].ToString());
```

```
        Console.WriteLine("The second value of the SortedList is " +
ar[2].ToString());
        Console.WriteLine("The third value of the SortedList is " +
ar[3].ToString());

        Console.Read();
    }
  }
}
```

In the above program:

- We can see that each element consists of a key and value.

- We can then access each value of the sorted list by providing the key as the index.

With this program, the output is as follows:

The first value of the SortedList is One

The second value of the SortedList is Two

The third value of the SortedList is Three

The SortedList class has a variety of operations that can be performed. Let's look at each one of these operations in more detail.

9.8 SortedList Operations

The section below provides the details of the various operations available for sorted lists.

Table 6: SortedList Operations

Function	Description
Count	This is used to get the number of elements in the SortedList
Clears()	This is used to remove all the elements in the SortedList
ContainsKey()	This is used to see if the SortedList contains a particular key
ContainsValue()	This is used to see if the SortedList contains a particular value
IndexOfKey()	This is used to get the index location of a particular key
IndexOfValue()	This is used to get the index location of a particular value
Remove()	This is used to remove an object from the SortedList
RemoveAt()	This is used to remove an object from the SortedList at a particular index position

9.8.1 Count Property

This property is used to get the number of elements in the sorted list.

Example 60: The program below is used to showcase the way to use the count property.

```
using System;
```

```
using System.Collections;
namespace Demo
{
    class Program
    {
        // The main function
        static void Main(string[] args)
        {
            // Defining the SortedList
            SortedList ar = new SortedList();

            // Adding elements to the SortedList
            ar.Add(1,"One");
            ar.Add(2,"Two");
            ar.Add(3,"Three");

            Console.WriteLine("The number of elements in the
SortedList is " + ar.Count);
            Console.Read();
        }
    }
}
```

With this program, the output is as follows:

The number of elements in the SortedList is 3

9.8.2 Clears Function

This function is used to remove all the elements in the sorted list.

Example 61: This program showcases the clears function.

```
using System;
using System.Collections;
namespace Demo
{
    class Program
    {
        // The main function
        static void Main(string[] args)
        {
            // Defining the SortedList
            SortedList ar = new SortedList();

            // Adding elements to the SortedList
            ar.Add(1, "One");
            ar.Add(2, "Two");
            ar.Add(3, "Three");
            Console.WriteLine("The number of elements in the
SortedList is " + ar.Count);

            // Clearing all the elements of the list
            ar.Clear();
            Console.WriteLine("The number of elements in the
SortedList is " + ar.Count);

            Console.Read();
        }
    }
}
```

With this program, the output is as follows:

The number of elements in the SortedList is 3

The number of elements in the SortedList is 0

9.8.3 ContainsKey Function

This function is used to determine if the sorted list contains a particular key.

Example 62: The following program is used to show how to use the ContainsKey function.

```
using System;
using System.Collections;
namespace Demo
{
  class Program
  {
    // The main function
    static void Main(string[] args)
    {
      // Defining the SortedList
      SortedList ar = new SortedList();

      // Adding elements to the SortedList
      ar.Add(1, "One");
      ar.Add(2, "Two");
      ar.Add(3, "Three");

      Console.WriteLine("Does the SortedList contain the key 3 " +
ar.ContainsKey(3));
      Console.Read();
    }
  }
}
```

With this program, the output is as follows:

Does the SortedList contain the key 3 True

9.8.4 ContainsValue Function

This function is used to determine if the sorted list contains a particular value.

Example 63: The program below is used to showcase the ContainsValue function.

```
using System;
using System.Collections;
namespace Demo
{
  class Program
  {
    // The main function
    static void Main(string[] args)
    {
      // Defining the SortedList
      SortedList ar = new SortedList();

      // Adding elements to the SortedList
      ar.Add(1, "One");
      ar.Add(2, "Two");
      ar.Add(3, "Three");

      Console.WriteLine("Does the SortedList contain the Value
Three " + ar.ContainsValue("Three"));

      Console.Read();
    }
  }
}
```

With this program, the output is as follows:

Does the SortedList contain the Value Three True

9.8.5 IndexOfKey Function

This function is used to get the index location of a particular key.

Example 64: The next program is used to show the way to use the IndexOfKey function.

```
using System;
using System.Collections;
namespace Demo
{
    class Program
    {
        // The main function
        static void Main(string[] args)
        {
            // Defining the SortedList
            SortedList ar = new SortedList();

            // Adding elements to the SortedList
            ar.Add(1, "One");
            ar.Add(2, "Two");
            ar.Add(3, "Three");

            Console.WriteLine("The index value of the key 3 is" +
ar.IndexOfKey(3));
            Console.Read();
        }
    }
}
```

With this program, the output is as follows:

The index value of the key 3 is 2

9.8.6 IndexOfValue Function

This function is used to get the index location of a particular value.

Example 65: This program shows how to use the IndexOfValue function.

```
using System;
using System.Collections;

namespace Demo
{
    class Program
    {
        // The main function
        static void Main(string[] args)
        {
            // Defining the SortedList
            SortedList ar = new SortedList();

            // Adding elements to the SortedList
            ar.Add(1, "One");
            ar.Add(2, "Two");
            ar.Add(3, "Three");

            Console.WriteLine("The index value of the key Three is" +
ar.IndexOfValue("Three"));

            Console.Read();
        }
    }
}
```

With this program, the output is as follows:

The index value of the key Three is 2

9.8.7 Remove Function

This function is used to remove an object from the sorted list.

Example 66: The following program showcases the remove function.

```
using System;
using System.Collections;

namespace Demo
{
    class Program
    {
        // The main function
        static void Main(string[] args)
        {
            // Defining the SortedList
            SortedList ar = new SortedList();

            // Adding elements to the SortedList
            ar.Add(1, "One");
            ar.Add(2, "Two");
            ar.Add(3, "Three");

            Console.WriteLine("Does the list contain the key 2 " +
ar.ContainsKey(2));
            ar.Remove(2);
            Console.WriteLine("Does the list contain the key 2 " +
ar.ContainsKey(2));

            Console.Read();
        }
    }
}
```

With this program, the output is as follows:

Does the list contain the key 2 True

Does the list contain the key 2 False

9.8.8 RemoveAt Function

This function is used to remove an object from the sorted list at a particular index position.

Example 67: The program below is used to show how to use the RemoveAt function.

```
using System;
using System.Collections;

namespace Demo
{
    class Program
    {
        // The main function
        static void Main(string[] args)
        {
            // Defining the SortedList
            SortedList ar = new SortedList();

            // Adding elements to the SortedList
            ar.Add(1, "One");
            ar.Add(2, "Two");
            ar.Add(3, "Three");

            Console.WriteLine("Does the list contain the key 2 " +
ar.ContainsKey(2));
            ar.RemoveAt(1);
            Console.WriteLine("Does the list contain the key 2 " +
ar.ContainsKey(2));
```

```
        Console.Read();
    }
  }
}
```

With this program, the output is as follows:

Does the list contain the key 2 True

Does the list contain the key 2 False

10. Generics

Generics allow the passing of data types to a method or class at runtime. Say we wanted to have a method that could perform operations on a range of data types and we didn't want to write the method several times. This is where generics would come in.

Let's look at an example of this using the Display method.

Example 68: The following program showcases the way to define multiple methods that achieve the same purpose.

```
using System;
using System.Collections;

namespace Demo
{
  class Program
  {
    // Display method for Integers
    public static void Add(int i)
{
Console.WriteLine("The value is " + i);
}

    // Display method for double numbers
      public static void Add(double i)
```

```
    {
    Console.WriteLine("The value is " + i);
    }

        // The main function
        static void Main(string[] args)
        {
            Display(1);
            Display(1.1);
            Console.Read();
        }
    }
}
```

With this program, the output is as follows:

The value is 1

The value is 1.1

Now in the above program, we are creating two methods that perform the same function of adding two numbers. However, we need to create two methods, one for the integer type and the other for the double data type. Let's see how we can make this program more generic by using the 'Generic' data type.

Example 69: The next program shows how to use the generic data type.

```
using System;
using System.Collections.Generic;
namespace Demo
{
    class Program
    {
        // Generic Display method
        public static void Display<T>(T i)
```

```
    {
        Console.WriteLine(" The value is " + i);
    }

        // The main function
        static void Main(string[] args)
        {
            // Calling the generic with the data type
            Display<int>(1);
            Display<double>(1.1);

            Console.Read();
        }
    }
}
```

With this program, the output is as follows:

The value is 1

The value is 1.1

10.1 Generic Classes

Classes can also be generic. The syntax declaration of a generic class is given below.

```
public class classname<T>
```

In this code, 'classname' is the name of the class. Let's look at an example of a generic class.

Example 70: The program below showcases the way to use the generic class.

```
using System;
using System.Collections.Generic;

namespace Demo
{
    // Generic class
    public class GenericSet<T>
    {
        private T[] array;
        public GenericSet(int size)
        {
            array = new T[size + 1];
        }
        public T getItem(int index)
        {
            return array[index];
        }
        public void setItem(int index, T value)
        {
            array[index] = value;
        }
    }
    class Program
    {
        // The main function
        static void Main(string[] args)
        {

            GenericSet<int> gn=new GenericSet<int>(2);
            gn.setItem(1,1);
            gn.setItem(2,2);

            Console.WriteLine("The first item is " + gn.getItem(1));
            Console.WriteLine("The second item is " + gn.getItem(2));
```

126

```
        Console.Read();
    }
  }
}
```

With this program, the output is as follows:

The first item is 1

The second item is 2

11. Events

Events are used in C# to notify us when any change is made to an object of a particular class. This is normally used when designing graphic user applications.

Events need to be used along with Delegates. Let's look at the steps required when working with events:

- Create a delegate to the event.

- Define a class which will hold the event.

- Define a method which will be triggered by the event. Attach this event to the delegate.

- Create a method which will trigger the event. This event will actually be attached to the delegate.

Let's now look at a complete program with all of these steps.

Example 71: The following program is used to showcase the way to work with events.

```
using System;
using System.Collections.Generic;

namespace Demo
{
    public delegate string newDel(string str);
```

```
class EventClass
{
    event newDel MyEvent;
    public void TriggerEvent()
    {
        this.MyEvent += new newDel(this.mymethod);
    }

    public string mymethod(string var)
    {
        return "Hello " + var;
    }
}

class Program
{
    // The main function
    static void Main(string[] args)
    {
        EventClass evt = new EventClass();
        Console.WriteLine("" + evt.mymethod("World"));

        Console.Read();
    }
}
```

With this program, the output is as follows:

Hello World

12. Multithreading

Threads are used for concurrent programming. All systems are designed to run programs as threads, which can run concurrently. Hence programming languages also have the facility to support threaded programming. By running threads, one can run multiple code side by side, and get added results in a shorter duration of time.

In C#, there is a separate 'Thread' class available. The steps to work with threads are as follows:

- First define a method that will be called when the thread has started execution.

- Next use the 'ThreadStart' type to define a reference to the method.

- Define a thread with the 'Thread' class.

- Then attach the 'ThreadStart' type reference to the created object.

- Lastly, use the start function to start the thread.

Let's look at a simple example of how to create a thread and implement the above steps.

Example 72: This program is used to show how to create a thread.

```
using System;
using System.Threading;

namespace Demo
{
    class Program
    {
        // This method will be called by the thread
        public static void ThreadModule()
        {
            Console.WriteLine("The thread is starting");
        }

        // The main function
        static void Main(string[] args)
        {
            // Making a reference to the ThreadModule
            ThreadStart start = new ThreadStart(ThreadModule);

            // Creating a new thread
            Thread thd = new Thread(start);

            // Starting the thread
            thd.Start();

            Console.Read();
        }
    }
}
```

With this program, the output is as follows:

The thread is starting

132

There are various functions available with threads. Let's look at them in more detail.

Table 7: Thread Operations

Function	Description
isAlive	This property is used to see if the thread is still alive
Name	This property is used to get or set the name of the thread
Priority	This property is used to get or set the priority of the thread
ThreadState	This property is used to get the state of the thread

12.1 isAlive

This property is used to determine if a thread is still alive.

Example 73: The following program showcases how to use the isAlive property.

```
using System;
using System.Threading;

namespace Demo
{
  class Program
  {
    // This method will be called by the thread
    public static void ThreadModule()
    {
      Console.WriteLine("The thread is starting");
```

```
        }

        // The main function
        static void Main(string[] args)
        {
            // Making a reference to the ThreadModule
            ThreadStart start = new ThreadStart(ThreadModule);

            // Creating a new thread
            Thread thd = new Thread(start);

            // Starting the thread
            thd.Start();
            Console.WriteLine("Is the thread alive " + thd.IsAlive);

            Console.Read();
        }
    }
}
```

With this program, the output is as follows:

Is the thread alive True

The thread is starting

12.2 Name

This property is used to get or set the name of a thread.

Example 74: This program is used to show the way to use the name property.

```
using System;
using System.Threading;
```

```
namespace Demo
{
    class Program
    {
        // This method will be called by the thread
        public static void ThreadModule()
        {
            Console.WriteLine("The thread is starting");
        }

        // The main function
        static void Main(string[] args)
        {
            // Making a reference to the ThreadModule
            ThreadStart start = new ThreadStart(ThreadModule);

            // Creating a new thread
            Thread thd = new Thread(start);

            // Starting the thread
            thd.Name = "First Thread";
            thd.Start();
            Console.WriteLine("The name of the thread is " + thd.Name);

            Console.Read();
        }
    }
}
```

With this program, the output is as follows:

The name of the thread is First Thread

The thread is starting

12.3 Priority

This property is used to get or set the priority of a thread.

Example 75: The program below is used to showcase the priority property.

```
using System;
using System.Threading;
namespace Demo
{
  class Program
  {
    // This method will be called by the thread
    public static void ThreadModule()
    {
      Console.WriteLine("The thread is starting");
    }

    // The main function
    static void Main(string[] args)
    {
      // Making a reference to the ThreadModule
      ThreadStart start = new ThreadStart(ThreadModule);

      // Creating a new thread
      Thread thd = new Thread(start);

      // Starting the thread
      thd.Name = "First Thread";
      thd.Priority = ThreadPriority.Highest;
      thd.Start();
      Console.WriteLine("The priority of the thread is " +
thd.Priority);

      Console.Read();
    }
  }}
```

With this program, the output is as follows:

The priority of the thread is Highest
The thread is starting

12.4 ThreadState

This property is used to determine the state of a thread.

Example 76: The next program shows how to use the ThreadState property.

```
using System;
using System.Threading;

namespace Demo
{
    class Program
    {
        // This method will be called by the thread
        public static void ThreadModule()
        {
            Console.WriteLine("The thread is starting");
        }

        // The main function
        static void Main(string[] args)
        {
            // Making a reference to the ThreadModule
            ThreadStart start = new ThreadStart(ThreadModule);

            // Creating a new thread
            Thread thd = new Thread(start);

            // Starting the thread
```

```
      thd.Name = "First Thread";
      thd.Priority = ThreadPriority.Highest;
      thd.Start();
      Console.WriteLine("The state of the thread is " +
thd.ThreadState);

      Console.Read();
    }
  }
}
```

With this program, the output is as follows:

The state of the thread is Running

The thread is starting

13. Regular Expressions

A regular expression is used for pattern matching techniques. For example, if we have a string and we want to determine if the string is an email address, then we would use a pattern such as string@string.string to determine if it was a valid email address.

There are various patterns that can be constructed. For example, the dot character (.) is a very general pattern that can be used to match any character. The alphabetic set (a-z) can also be used to match all letters from 'a' to 'z'.

C# has support for regular expressions by using the 'Regex' class. Let's look at a simple program for regular expressions.

Example 77: The following program is used to showcase the way to use regular expressions.

```
using System;
using System.Text.RegularExpressions;

namespace Demo
{
    class Program
    {
        // The main function
        static void Main(string[] args)
```

```
    {
        String src = "Hello World";
        string pattern = @"Hello";

        Regex rgx = new Regex(pattern, RegexOptions.IgnoreCase);
    MatchCollection matches = rgx.Matches(src);
    if (matches.Count > 0)
    {
        foreach (Match m in matches)
        {
            Console.WriteLine(m);
        }
    }
        Console.Read();
        }
    }
}
```

In the above program we are:

- Specifying our source string, in order to look for pattern matches.

- Next, we state what pattern we want. In our example we want to find out if the word 'Hello' is in the source string.

- We then use the 'Regex' class with our pattern, and apply our source string.

- The output is a list of matches. We then display those matches accordingly.

With this program, the output is as follows:

Hello

Let's look at another example where we can use regular expressions to get digits that are embedded in a string.

Example 78: The following program also shows how to use regular expressions.

```
using System;
using System.Text.RegularExpressions;

namespace Demo
{
  class Program
  {
    static void Main(string[] args)
    {
      string input = "Let's have the number of 2000";

      Match m = Regex.Match(input, @"\d+");

      Console.WriteLine("The number in the string is " + m.Value);
      Console.ReadKey();
    }
  }
}
```

With this program, the output is as follows:

The number in the string is 2000

Once a match is found using regular expressions, we can also use the length and index property to get the length of the found string and the index in the source string where the match string was found.

Example 79: This program showcases how to use regular expressions with the length and index property.

```
using System;
using System.Text.RegularExpressions;
namespace ConsoleApp2
{
    class Program
    {
        static void Main(string[] args)
        {
            string input = "Let's have the number of 2000";

            Match m = Regex.Match(input, @"\d+");

            Console.WriteLine("The number in the string is " + m.Value);
            Console.WriteLine("The length of the derived value is " +
m.Length);
            Console.WriteLine("The index in the string where the value
was found is " + m.Index);

            Console.ReadKey();
        }
    }
}
```

With this program, the output is as follows:

The number in the string is 2000

The length of the derived value is 4

The index in the string where the value was found is 25

Conclusion

We have unfortunately reached the end of this guide. But as I always say, it doesn't mean your C# journey should end here. Practice as much as possible. This book was written not only to be a teaching guide, but also a reference manual. So remember to always keep it near, as you venture through this wonderful world of programming.

If you enjoyed this guide, and this series, be sure to look into the other programming languages I cover, such as Java. Its open source framework and compatibility has made it an extremely popular language. Java allows for its programs to run on virtually any platform via the Java Runtime Environment. It's one of the most versatile languages available today and favored for mobile development.

JAVA

Programming Basics for Absolute Beginners

a FREE Kindle Version with Paperback

About the Author

Nathan Clark is an expert programmer with nearly 20 years of experience in the software industry.

With a master's degree from MIT, he has worked for some of the leading software companies in the United States and built up extensive knowledge of software design and development.

Nathan and his wife, Sarah, started their own development firm in 2009 to be able to take on more challenging and creative projects. Today they assist high-caliber clients from all over the world.

Nathan enjoys sharing his programming knowledge through his book series, developing innovative software solutions for their clients and watching classic sci-fi movies in his free time.

Made in the USA
Middletown, DE
13 February 2019